Gene Autry and Roy Rogers: Ame

By Charles River Editors

A statue of Gene Autry in Palm Springs, Florida

About Charles River Editors

Charles River Editors provides superior editing and original writing services across the digital publishing industry, with the expertise to create digital content for publishers across a vast range of subject matter. In addition to providing original digital content for third party publishers, we also republish civilization's greatest literary works, bringing them to new generations of readers via ebooks.

Sign up here to receive updates about free books as we publish them, and visit Our Kindle Author Page to browse today's free promotions and our most recently published Kindle titles.

Introduction

Gene Autry (1907-1998)

"Music has been the better part of my career. Movies are wonderful fun and they give you a famous face. But how the words and melody are joined, how they come together out of air and enter the mind, this is art. Songs are forever." – Gene Autry

In the early 20th century, Westerns were one of the most popular genres in Hollywood, and one of the young stars at the forefront was Gene Autry, a Texan whose life story made him a natural to be the country's most famous "singing cowboy". Autry would become a symbol of masculinity and morality on screen during the 1930s, but it was effortless for someone who had already grown up riding horses to school.

Autry came of age at a time when the "singing cowboy" was at the apex of his popularity, and like his most famous successor, Roy Rogers, Autry actually got his start in show business as a singer. Even today, Autry might be best known for being a pioneer of country music and the author of Christmas hits "Here Comes Santa Claus", "Frosty the Snowman", and "Rudolph the Red-Nosed Reindeer". Autry would produce hundreds of recordings during his life, helping ensure the popularity of the country music genre and earning inductions into several related halls of fame.

Of course, the popularity of Autry's music and country music in general was bolstered by the fact that he became one of the biggest stars in Hollywood. After he was discovered in 1934, Autry made dozens of films and was still one of the industry's biggest moneymakers when he went off to fight in World War II. Though his movie career had already hit its peak by the time he returned, Autry used his popularity and his skills to transition into television, and he dabbled in all kinds of other ventures, including owning a radio station and professional sports teams. By the end of his long life and career, Autry could lay claim to being the only man with 5 stars on the Hollywood Walk of Fame for film, television, music, radio, and live performances.

Gene Autry and Roy Rogers examines the life and career of one of America's most famous singing cowboys. Along with pictures of important people, places, and events, you will learn about Gene Autry like never before.

Roy Rogers and Phyllis Brooks in *Silver Spurs* (1943).

Roy Rogers (1911-1998)

"I did pretty good for a guy who never finished high school and used to yodel at square dances." – Roy Rogers

In the early 20th century, Westerns were one of the most popular genres in Hollywood, and one of the young stars at the forefront was Roy Rogers, who had come from an Ohio farm to transform himself into a cowboy. Regardless of his background, Rogers certainly looked the part of the quintessential cowboy, along with his wife Dale Evans and his horse Trigger. His versatile singing and acting abilities made him successful both on radio and on the screen.

Rogers came of age at a time when the "singing cowboy" was at the apex of his popularity, and that was favorable because he actually got his start in show business as a singer. In the early '30s, he bounced around several groups as a country music singer before earning national attention as a member of the Sons of the Pioneers, who were signed to Decca and had a couple of hits. As a result, when he first appeared in movies in 1935, it was usually in bit roles that required singing, but when Gene Autry threatened to quit acting in 1938, Rogers was viewed as a suitable replacement for lead roles. As it turned out, he became the premiere "singing cowboy" in Autry's stead, and from 1939-1954, he was one of the Top 10 Western stars in Hollywood, and a Top 10 movie star overall during some of those years.

As Rogers evolved into the "King of the Cowboys", he became a pop culture icon, and he was shrewd enough to capitalize on his image. All sorts of Roy Rogers merchandise hit stores, from action figures to comic strips, and Rogers even banked on the popularity of his horse Trigger by featuring him enough to make the horse a household name as well. Even today, people can find the name Roy Rogers all over the place, if only because he eventually had his name lent to a popular fast food chain in later years.

Even as his movie career inevitably tailed off, Rogers remained popular enough to host a television show in the '60s with his wife, and though it was only on for a short while, the show's theme song, "Happy Trails", is still well-known today. Rogers continued to appear on television and was involved with a production company in later years, the capstone on a career that saw him earn 3 stars on the Hollywood Walk of Fame and induction into both the Western Performers Hall of Fame and Country Music Hall of Fame.

Gene Autry and Roy Rogers chronicles the life and career of one of America's most famous actors. Along with pictures of important people, places, and events, you will learn about the "King of the Cowboys" like never before.

Gene Autry and Roy Rogers: America's Two Favorite Singing Cowboys

About Charles River Editors

Introduction

Bibliography

compose new material to perform. Autry claimed, "Everything began with a man named Jimmy Long…Though he was considerably older than I, we shared an interest in … music, and even wrote a few songs together." Autry also described how they went about writing songs together: "I tried to write songs—you don't just write a song right quick, you fool around and work with that song to try to get a good one. You have to keep going over and over and over it and see if you can't really write a song that means a lot."

The two men would become even closer when Autry married Long's niece, Ina May Spivey, in 1932, and according to one friend, their marriage was one made in heaven: "She loved everything she did for Gene. He didn't realize how much she loved him, I don't think. She told me how they got married on the quick, and that she had a tear in her dress, but they got married anyway. Afterward, she picked out what she wanted in a wedding ring…she got a nice one. They didn't mix with the movie crowd in Hollywood much at all. They never put on any high-falutin' stuff."

Autry is famous across the world as a singer, but his songwriting was a crucial aspect of his early success, and he later relayed a story about his big decision to take a chance on performing music professionally: "The job [with the railroad] gave me free transportation on the railroad but I didn't have any place to go, until one night a cattle man from Tulsa listened to me singin' a song I'd made up myself, 'count of I'd played the old ones plumb out. 'Son,' he said to me, 'my sister's got herself a radio, an' some o' the singin' comes outa the thing ain't no better than that tune you're wranglin'. Why don't you git yourself up to Noow York? I hear as how they even pay folks for singin' up there.'"

Having already heard the same from Gene Austin, Autry took the man's words to heart and did "get himself up to New York." Once there, he began to pound the pavement like so many other talented people did before and after him, but despite how many times he tried to find someone willing to give him a chance to perform, he kept having no luck. Finally, he got his big break: "I was over at Victor trying to get an audition and there was a fellow, Leonard Joy, he was the A&R director at that time, and he heard me and said, 'Where are you from?' and I told him, 'Oklahoma.' And he said, 'Well, you know Johnny Marvin…he's one of our top artists and he's from Oklahoma. You have that twang about your voice, you sound very much like some of those fellas,' and I said, 'I've never met Johnny, but I've met his mother.' And he said, 'Well, fine, I'll give you his number and you call him.' So I called him and he said, 'Look, my brother Frankie is living in New York at some little hotel and you two ought to get together.'"

Johnny Marvin

Frankie Marvin would prove to be Autry's partner, friend, and the key that would open the doors of fame, but at the time they met, they were just two young men having fun in the big city. According to Autry, "We'd go to some pool halls and play pool, and he knew where there were a few speakeasies around there, and we'd go up and have a bottle of beer…That was before Prohibition was repealed. And we got to be very close buddies."

FRANK MARVIN

Frankie Marvin

Chapter 2: Len Slye and Duck Run

"I was born in Cincinnati, but was raised on a farm in a little place called Duck Run. I went to school there and got two years of high school before I had to go to work. The Depression was coming on and it was hard for anyone to get a job. I worked with my dad at the shoe factory in Cincinnati." - Roy Rogers

Leonard Franklin Slye was born on November 5, 1911 in Cincinnati, Ohio, a far cry from the wide open spaces his name would come to represent. He was not born on a spacious ranch but in a walk-up tenement on Second Street, and when the tenement was torn down and Riverfront

Stadium erected in its place, he would tell people that he was born near second base. Len was the third child and only son of Andy and Mattie Slye. Andy worked for the United States Shoe Company, while Mattie spent her days trying to keep up with Len and his siblings, which came to include three sisters. Mattie was slowed in her efforts by the long-term effects of the polio she suffered as a child.

Before little Len was a year old, Andy and his brother Will finished work on a houseboat they had been renovating, and in July 1912, "Andy's Ark" left Cincinnati and sailed down the Ohio River to Andy's family home in Portsmouth, Ohio. Len would learn to walk and talk on that houseboat while his father worked for a nearby shoe factory, and he might have grown to adulthood on that little house on the river if he had not been found at the age of five wondering along behind an ice wagon. Concerned with keeping better track of their mischievous son, Andy and Mattie decided to move their family inland. Eventually, they were able to sail their houseboat up a narrow river created by the Great Flood of 1913 and hauled it on to land about 12 miles outside Portsmouth.

Their new home was called Duck Run, and it provided a comfortable living place for everyone while Andy continued to work at the shoe factory. Due to the distance between Duck Run and the factory, Andy lived in Portsmouth, so he was only able to return home twice a month, and though he was still just 6 years old, Len considered himself the man of the family and soon mastered farming skills such as plowing and planting. He hunted with a slingshot to put meat on the table, and he helped care for the family's chickens, pigs and mule. He even learned how to defend himself against a cruel schoolmaster.

A picture of Duck Run taken by Don O'Brien.

From a very young age, Len was drawn to music, as was the rest of his family. Len and his siblings all played musical instruments, with Len's specialty being the mandolin and guitar. Len also sang well, a skill his musical parents recognized and encouraged. Though there were few opportunities for the boy to sing professionally, he made sure to take advantage of those that came up, and before long, he was in demand to call square dances or to sing at church socials.

To supplement his talents and income, Len even learned to yodel after his father had saved enough money to buy an early cylinder-style phonograph with a number of cylinders. One of these had a Swiss yodeler, and Len listened to it over and over again until he mastered the style and timing of the man on the cylinder. Mattie and his sisters also mastered yodeling, allowing them to communicate with each other across great distances. The family worked out different signals to indicate what each wanted the other to know.

Len also learned how to ride the horse his father gave him for Christmas the year he turned 11. In fact, not only did he learn to ride the horse, he also taught the horse to do tricks. His horse was dear to him, but his family dearer; unlike many actors who would look back on unhappy or even abusive childhoods, Roy Rogers would speak fondly of his memories growing up in Duck Run. But times were still hard financially, so when Len was a sophomore in high school, his parents decided to make a change. They moved the family back to Cincinnati in the hopes that both father and son could find work.

In 1928, a 10th grade education was considered plenty for the average boy, so Len dropped out of school to get a job with his father at the United States Shoe Company. Though the family was happy to have the extra $25.00 a week he earned in the insole department, his mother wanted him to go back to school. In an effort to placate both parents, he decided to take high school classes at night, but after a long day of work, he found that he just could not stay awake through the long classes. After one particular episode earned him ridicule, he dropped out again, this time for good.

In 1929, Len's oldest sister, Mary, got married and moved across the country to sunny California. Neither Len nor his father was happy living and working in the big city. With nothing tying them to Ohio, the family pooled their resources and began the long journey to California. Rogers later recalled, "I got up one morning and dad said, 'let's quit our jobs today and go out to see Mary in California'. We were a close family and really missed my older sister. We talked about her all the time. Well, I was just thrilled to death. I told him I had about ninety dollars and thought that was enough for gas. We started packing and were rolling out in about three days."

Their trip proved to be quite an adventure, thanks to the poor condition of their car. Rogers remembered, "Oh, it was a pistol. We were in an old 1923 Dodge. We had several flat tires. It took us two weeks to come out here. Of course, ninety bucks bought a lot of gas back then. I think we picked up Route 66 somewhere around St. Louis. I remember that we burned out the bearings in New Mexico. In those days, they didn't have places where you could buy bearings and things like that. We had to go out to a junkyard and find another Dodge like ours and take out the bearings. That cost us a couple of days." In case they needed more parts, they decided to buy the entire junk car and tow it behind them as a sort of mobile auto parts store.

After several weeks of driving all day and sleeping on the side of the road at night, the family arrived in California, and Len and his father were pleased to discover that Mary's husband had already lined up work for them driving gravel trucks. Though it was hot and dirty work, they found it a refreshing change from being trapped in a stuffy factory all day. After four months in California, they returned to Cincinnati but did not stay there long. They had found a new home, they felt, and they moved permanently to California in 1931.

Len and the family initially liked California, but they soon found that living there was not as nice as visiting it. The company they had worked for during their first visit went bankrupt, so Len and his father were forced to take jobs as migrant workers. Rogers would later explain, "For the whole summer of 1931 we picked peaches near Bakersfield in the San Joaquin Valley. When we came back (to Los Angeles), there weren't any jobs. This was during the Depression and there just wasn't any work. That's how I got into show business, really."

Except for spoiled peaches, there was little to eat in the camp. Once, when Len manage to kill a rabbit, he and his father cooked it over an open fire, but before it was done, they were surrounded by hungry children begging for a bite. While the children ate the rabbit, the men played their guitars and sang to them. When the summer ended and there was no more produce to be picked, the family moved back to Los Angeles. Andy planned to get a job at a shoe factory, but Len, now 20 years old, wanted to try his hand at something better: he wanted to go into show business. He and his cousin Stanley, who had come to California with them, teamed up to form the "Slye Brothers", but when that didn't work out, the two split up and Len joined "Uncle Tom Murray's Hollywood Hillbillies".

After Uncle Tom Murray's Hollywood Hillbillies didn't pan out either, Len considered giving up, but his sister Mary encouraged him to try one more venue. He later noted, "There was a program on a radio station in Inglewood called the Midnight Frolic. It was an amateur show and anyone could go on. It was on the air from midnight to six in the morning. My sister said I should go on the show. She took me up there and when they called my name, I just froze. Mary touched me on the shoulder and said, 'Now you get up there and sing.' I sang a couple of songs. I don't to this day remember what songs I sang. I was so scared." Fortunately, his one radio performance proved to be what he needed to break into show business: "About three days later this guy called and asked if I wanted to join a group he called the 'Rocky Mountaineers'. It was better than picking peaches. I didn't get any more money, really. But, it was easier work and I enjoyed it."

The group was made up of several men who played instruments, but they felt they needed to add a singer and Len was happy to oblige. They started performing together on a radio show in Long Beach, but Len soon felt that they would have a better band if they added another performer to sing harmony with him. The group put out a classified ad that read, ""Yodeler for old-time act, to travel. Tenor preferred." Eventually, the group hired Bob Nolan, a singer/songwriter then making his living working as a lifeguard. Len and Bob were soon joined by Bill Nichols, completing their happy band, but Bob would soon drop out and be replaced by Tim Spencer. Rogers explained, "I was the only singer in the Rocky Mountaineers. Bob Nolan joined me and later Tim Spencer. We became the Pioneer Trio. When we got to KFWB radio, they picked the three of us off the Texas Outlaw program and put us on staff."

Bob Nolan

Over the next two years, the group would continue to try different combinations of talent, names and music styles. In June 1933, they began their first music tour, traveling around the southwestern United States as the "O-Bar-O Cowboys", but Rogers would later admit to a reporter, "We starved to death on that trip. We ate jack rabbits; we ate anything we could get to eat." The tour proved to be a disappointment, both financially and professionally, as few people turned out to see the unheard of band, but on a personal level, it proved to be a huge success for Len. During a radio performance in Roswell, New Mexico, the boys began to tell the man interviewing them about their hopes for the future, and it soon became clear that most of their dreams simply centered on having enough good food to eat. A Mrs. Wilkins was listening that night and felt sorry for the young men, some of whom seemed to be about the age of her own children, so she called in and promised that if Len would sing "The Swiss Yodel" the following evening, she would bring him and the rest of the group two lemon pies. Len sang the song and she showed up, not just with the pies, but with her pretty daughter Arline. As much as Len liked the pie, he liked Arline even more and happily accepted Mrs. Wilkins' invitation to join them for a fried chicken dinner the next day.

When Len returned to Los Angeles, it was with Arline Wilkins' address in his pocket. The two began writing to each other, with Len sharing his frustrations over the way people were leaving the group. He also told her about his efforts with "Jack and His Texas Outlaws", and how that petered out. He subsequently shared his plans to form his own group, and how he'd been in touch with Bob Nolan and Tim Spencer. The three men decided to give show business one more try, this time billing themselves as the "Pioneers Trio".

After asking around, the trio finally landed an audition with KFWB, and by that point, they had worked hard to master their music and felt that they had a good chance of being hired. They sang their hearts out, all while watching the blank faces of the station's general manager, Jerry King, and its announcer, Harry Hall, as they listened. They had just begun their big yodeling number when King left, and according to Nolan, "our hearts fell to our feet." It was only after they finished their song that they learned King had ordered Hall to hire them before he left.

Being signed by KFWB was a good start, but the station could not afford to pay them, so the only work the three could get consisted of voluntary gigs on KFWB and other small radio stations. Their hard work paid off once they began to get requests to sing at local events and venues, and the radio station eventually grew so afraid of losing their services that it started paying them each $35 a week to perform. Although they still called themselves the Pioneers Trio, the radio announcer renamed them the "Sons of the Pioneers", saying they were all too young to be pioneers themselves. The name stuck, and it would become synonymous with Roy Rogers for the rest of his life.

As is often the case, success built upon success, and in August 1934, the quartet, which now included fiddle player Hugh Farr, made their first record, "Tumbling Tumbleweeds", which featured "Moonlight on the Prairie" on the flipside. They made one cent for every record sold.

Chapter 3: Gene Autry the Music Star or Gene Autry the Movie Star?

Autry in *Oh, Susanna!* (1936)

"It occurs to me that music, with the possible exception of riding a bull, is the most uncertain way to make a living I know. In either case you can get bucked off, thrown, stepped on, trampled--if you get on at all. At best, it is a short and bumpy ride." – Gene Autry

"I happened to come along in an era when movies were changing. That was about 1934. There was a break between the great silent screen stars - Buck Jones, Tom Mix and Hoot Gibson - and the new crop that was to come along. I was the first of the singing cowboys. If I'd come into pictures five years earlier or five years later, I might not have succeeded. As I look over my life, I'd say the most important thing is to be at the right place at the right time." - Gene Autry

After auditioning for Victor, Autry was sent home to gain some experience because, they told him, he had plenty of talent but was not what they were looking for. As a result, he and Long began singing together wherever they could find a station that would let them perform, and in 1929, they recorded their first record: a single with "My Dreaming of You" on one side and "My Alabama" on the other. The songs were played across the Midwest and ultimately won Autry a contract with Columbia Records, as well as his own radio show broadcast out of Chicago, Illinois.

By this time, Autry had changed his first name from Orvon to Gene, and while many believe it was in honor of Gene Austin, the reason for his choice technically remains a mystery. Regardless, in the earliest days of his career, Gene Autry focused primarily on a "hillbilly" style of music that was characterized by nasally tones consistent with the speech patterns found in Tennessee and Oklahoma. Written during the last years of Prohibition, the tunes focused on bootlegging, loose women, and deception, themes that were quite different from the more family-friendly "God and country" style of music he would later adopt.

In 1932, Autry and Long released their first major hit, "That Silver-Haired Daddy of Mine." The two collaborated on both writing and performing the number, which became an instant hit and brought them national attention. With that, Autry was soon approached about making a movie for Mascot Pictures and appearing as one of a quartet of singing cowboys. At first, he resisted the offer, later noting, "I knew very little about pictures. I was really green. In fact, I had never been around a studio—I didn't know anything about a camera." Once curiosity finally got the best of him, he agreed to appear in a movie entitled *In Old Santa Fe* (1934).

Autry would be one of the biggest icons of the Western genre, but his first movie almost ended up on a back room shelf, especially after Autry saw the first film of his performance. He later complained, "I moved like my parts needed oiling, and I didn't like the way I looked or sounded." He also told his wife, "I don't think I'll ever be worth a damn in pictures. I don't think I'm the type." However, the studio disagreed and went forward with the movie's release, and it soon became a hit with critics and fans alike, with one theatre owner telling a reporter that it was "[o]ne of the best westerns I've ever run...Good story, plenty of thrills, comedy, and some good music and singing by Gene Autry and his band. This is the kind of Western that pleases my patrons."

With *In Old Santa Fe's* success, Autry seemingly faced a very important decision over whether to continue with a singing career or attempt to become a movie star. While trying to make up his mind, he contacted one of his heroes, Tom Mix, and "asked his advice as to whether I should stick to Westerns or try becoming a singing star in regular pictures." Mix's response changed Autry's future: "Gene, the life of an ordinary star may only be five years, but a Western star can go on forever—it's like life insurance." After talking to Mix, Autry moved to Hollywood to try his hand in the film industry, later writing, "I recall when I left WLS in Chicago I was making in the neighborhood of $350 a week and I went to Hollywood at $100 a week. I realized it was much less than what I was making, but I thought that the future held much more for me to earn than it would have been to remain where I was in Chicago."

Once he moved west, Autry subsequently went on to make *Melody Ranch* (1935), the film that also gave its name to his radio show just a few years later. Like all good cowboy heroes, Autry had his own horse, girl, and chosen sidekick. His faithful sidekick's name was Lester Burnette, but most people called him Smiley, and Autry later admitted, "I've always said that Smiley certainly was responsible for a lot of my success."

Smiley Burnette

Autry performing with Smiley Burnette in the movie *In Old Santa Fe*

Meanwhile, Autry's most famous horse was Champion, and Champion went on to be featured in both movies and stage shows. Once the original Champion died, Autry's subsequent horses would also take the name Champion, and they were cared for by Johnny Agee, who had once cared for Tom Mix's horses. Autry explained, "Johnny went to work for me taking care of all my horses. He worked the original Champion, too, as to certain tricks he had to do in pictures. When I went on rodeos, I used Lindy because he looked like Champion. He had four stockings and a bald face. He was truly one of the finest animals I ever owned and perhaps the most talented and easiest to train of all my Champions. I used him primarily for my stage appearances and in parades because he was even-tempered and well behaved."

A statue of Autry and a horse in Los Angeles, California

Champion's screen credit in *Oh, Susanna!* (1936)

Autry also had his favorite leading lady, though that role would be enjoyed by several different women through the years. The first was a pretty brunette named Ann Rutherford, who later revealed a secret about Autry that few of his fans would have believed: he was not a natural horseman. Autry himself later joked about some of the elements that went into his star image: "I couldn't shoot a man in the back. I couldn't take a drink at a bar. They would have run me out of town...I could never have played scenes like where The Sundance Kid kicks the guy in the nuts or anything like Clint Eastwood does."

Of course, he made up for any perceived deficiencies in other ways, and as Rutherford noted in 1936, Autry "was getting acquainted with the fine points of riding, and he got real good at it. He looked wonderful in the saddle...You know, up to that time, many of the cowboys looked grubby—but Gene was in the white hat, and he also sang so pretty...Gene had what my mother used to called a real 'come out of the kitchen voice'. When he sang on radio, if you were out in the kitchen and you heard him you knew right away it was!"

Ann Rutherford

In 1935, Autry made the first in a 12-part series called *The Phantom Empire*. The first film installment was 30 minutes long, with the following 11 being 20 minutes each. It was based on an unusual combination of Western and science fiction genres, with Autry playing a cowboy who discovers a secret world living under his ranch. According to one critic, it played a central role in shaping cinematic history: "Had there been no *Phantom Empire*, it is doubtful if there would have been a *Flash Gordon* from Universal in 1936, or a *Buck Rogers* (1939)...nor would science fiction have become so much a staple of serial production for the next ten years."

Not long after Autry joined Mascot, the company was bought out by Republic Pictures, and Autry would appear in 44 movies for the company over the next five years. He also quickly became one of the most sought after stars in Hollywood, with the *Los Angeles Times* proclaiming, "Probably the largest percentage of fan mail that enters Hollywood is received by Western stars, even though they might make only a few pictures each year. Their products gross large returns. Gene Autry, while somewhat of a newcomer to the Western ranks, is already among the topnotchers, mainly for the reason that he brings to the screen an important part of the range that was heretofore missing—he combines a pleasing singing voice along with his ability as a Western actor—and singing Westerns have been scarce."

Autry's next film was *Tumbling Tumbleweeds* (1935), and decades later, a film historian wrote, "Gene Autry's first Western for Republic Pictures—indeed, it's regarded as the very first 'singing cowboy' Western ever—is one of his best, a very entertaining programmer that crams a lot of entertainment into its short-and-to-the-point 58 minutes. It's more a Western with music than a typical Gene Autry Western; although the basic components for the dozens of musical Westerns Autry would subsequently make for the studio are on display, it's pleasingly rough around the edges, without the formula blandness that would quickly permeate his films."

By 1936, Autry was considered one of the Top Ten Money-Making Western Stars in a poll done by the *Motion Picture Herald*, and he would remain on that list every year through 1954 except for the four years he served in the Army Air Corps during World War II. From 1937 until he left for the war, he would hold the top spot, and after he returned from serving his country, he would remain in the number two spot for nearly a decade. One of the movies that made and kept Autry famous was *Red River Valley* (1936). Taking its title from a haunting folk song written sometime in the last half of the 19th century, it starred Autry as a man of principle once more righting wrongs done against the innocent and helpless. Filming it proved to be a challenge, as Autry would later explain: "We were right out in the desert. We shot a lot of it along the Colorado River, and I did a big fight on the dam, and the dam was very slippery. It had kind of a moss over the spillway, and I darned near drowned in that thing too. When I went over the spillway, why, it was in the wintertime and I couldn't get my breath, and I had kind of a tough time there…When you go over a spillway in a dam, there's a great pressure there and you really have to swim to get out of it."

Although he was now a movie star, Autry continued to write many of the songs he performed on screen, and he often found unusual sources of inspiration. For instance, he told the following story about writing "You're the Only Star (In My Blue Heaven)" in 1936: "I found myself receiving love letters from a lady in Iowa…She had developed the notion that I was singing to her, just to her, and the letters, reeking with Gypsy Rose perfume, would begin: 'Gene, darling, I heard the song you sang to me last night and I understood'…In the last one I received, she described being alone that night. After hearing me sing she walked outside, stood on the porch, and gazed at the evening sky. 'I looked at the stars in the heavens," she wrote. 'I saw millions of them. But you are the only star in my blue heaven.'"

In 1937, Autry starred in *Boots and Saddles* (1937), but it was not considered one of his best efforts. According to *The New York Times* movie critic Bosley Crowther, "Its star is that personable and pleasant-voiced singing cowboy, Gene Autry, who is said to have one of the most formidable fan followings in the nation, but its supporting musical interludes, full of Latin-American hip swinging, range from indifferent to bad, and its story, involving Gene's effort to sell horses to the army, in order to save the old 'rawnch' for its youthful English owner, is one of the least justifiable of the year, especially as a libretto for livestock."

That same year, Autry made one of his few forays into national politics: "Back in 1937, Mr. Sam Rayburn, who was my congressman from my district in Texas, called and said there was a young man down there from Austin runnin' for Congress and could use a little help...So I went down with my guitar and a couple of musicians and we stayed with young Lyndon maybe two weeks." That Lyndon was none other than Lyndon Johnson, who rose up the ranks of Texas politics and ultimately became president in 1963.

In 1937, Autry became an international sensation when the first Gene Autry Fan Club was founded in Great Britain. Though smaller than many similar clubs in the United States, the club published its own newsletter, whimsically named *The Westerner*, and Autry got to meet many of his fans in person when he took his live *Gene Autry Show* on tour in England in 1939. One of the highlights of this show was Gene performing his new song, "Back in the Saddle Again." Co-written by Autry and Ray Whitely, it would go on to become his theme song for the rest of his life, and more than 50 years later, it would be inducted into the Grammy Hall of Fame and also be voted one of the 100 best songs of the 20th century. The haunting lyrics will forever be associated with Autry.

"I'm back in the saddle again, out where a friend is a friend
Where the longhorn cattle feed, On the lowly gypsum weed
Back in the saddle again.

Ridin' the range once more totin' my old 44
Where you sleep out every night and the only law is right
Back in the saddle again."

Autry was a huge hit in England, perhaps more so because the war clouds were obviously gathering in the country at that time. He would later describe the reception he received in London: "I never saw so many people in my life. The whole front of the theater and the streets were all blocked and people everywhere. Well, Bill Saal was quite a PR guy, and he had a lot of cameramen with him...He'd said, 'I want you to jump off the stage and just walk up the middle of the aisle because I want to get your picture outside with all of that crowd.' Well, that's exactly what I did. I went outside...but I couldn't get out of that mob, so finally Bill yelled, 'come on up here,' and I got up on top of this small Austin convertible car...and this bobby came up to Bill Saal and said, 'Is this your car?' and Bill said, 'Hell, yes, get away from it and don't bother me!' I often wondered what the owner of that automobile thought when he came back and saw the condition of it!" Autry was at the peak of his career, but he tried to remain modest about his accomplishments: "I know I'm no great actor, and I'm not a great rider, and I'm not a great singer, but whatever it is I'm doing, they like it. So I'm going to keep doing it as long as I can."

After he returned from England, Autry premiered a weekly radio show on CBS called *Gene Autry's Melody Ranch*, and it ran for 16 years, albeit in a shortened format when Autry was away fighting during World War II. According to John Dutton, "[The] show changed little over the years. It featured a slightly sophisticated version of his 1929 act—Autry stories and songs, projected in a campfire atmosphere. Autry told his listeners that his broadcasts were coming directly from his home, Melody Ranch, in the San Fernando Mountains. He surrounded himself with a cast of regular foot-stompers ... The music was decidedly Western, with heavy accordion emphasis. There was usually one 'Cowboy Classic' by Autry. [Pat] Buttram's acts were inserted for comic relief and consisted mainly of back-and-forth banter with Autry...The highlight of each show, at least for the juvenile listeners, came when Autry told a 10- to 15-minute story, fully dramatized, of some recent adventure."

Buttram

The show always featured Autry singing at least one of his famous songs, and it usually included some sort of Western themed story starring Autry and his sidekicks. Champion was on Autry's show, and he often appeared on Champion's show, *The Adventures of Champion*. Naturally, these shows appealed primarily to a younger audience, and though he and Ina would never have children of their own, Autry always felt a close kinship with his youngest fans and a strong sense of responsibility for their moral upbringing. Just after the show began, he told a reporter, "…the radio show I am doing is not a sophisticated program and probably a lot of the boys in the city won't enjoy it, but the thing I am trying to do more than anything else is to keep the program down to earth, and especially so the kids will like it. I want to concentrate on trying to point out the value of Americanism and what America should mean to everyone in these days where there is so much communism and other isms going so strong in this country. I feel we cannot go too strong on preaching this to the people, and I think the best way to do this is playing particularly to the kids and teaching them Americanism while they are young."

Autry was not the only one concerned about America's future; most of Europe was already embroiled in World War II, and it seemed inevitable to many that America would eventually join the war as well. While politicians and society in general agonized over whether to join the war, Hollywood was busy making movies to support the values that the country held dear. Of course, few genres represented American values like Westerns, as noted by movie critic Douglas Churchill in *The New York Times* in late 1940: "The Western is employed as the logical medium in which to expound the American philosophy and to show that right thinking, clean living, and a devotion to duty are the ingredients necessary to success. That some of the outdoors pictures will make no attempt to conceal the propaganda goes without saying: most, however, will strive for adroitness and preach in general terms and by inference." No one was surprised when Autry became a leader in this patriotic movement.

A poster featuring Autry in *Home on the Prairie* (1939)

Chapter 4: Roy Rogers Goes From Backup to Star

"I'm an introvert at heart and show business, even though I've loved it so much, has always been hard for me." - Roy Rogers

In 1930s Hollywood, there was often a natural progression from performing in public to making movies, because while there were never enough roles for every aspiring actor, truly talented people were also in short supply. Thus, in 1935, the Sons of the Pioneers began making cameo appearances in movies. In most of their earliest films, the band is not even mentioned in the credits, but they were seen at least briefly in *Slightly Static* (1935) and *Gallant Defender*

(1935). When they were credited at all, the future Roy Rogers was still billed as Len Slye, which was the case in *The Old Homestead* (1935), *Way Up Thar* (1935), and *The Mysterious Avenger* (1936).

Thanks to their roles in movies, the Sons of the Pioneers began to develop more of a national following. In 1936, the State of Texas invited them to perform at its Centennial celebration, which provided Len the opportunity to make a stop in Roswell on his way to the performance and marry Arline. The wedding was small and held at her parents' home, and the honeymoon consisted of the Texas trip.

Meanwhile, Len continued to appear in movies, including appearing in five more uncredited roles in 1936, and in 1937, the Sons of the Pioneers signed a contract with Columbia Pictures to appear in a series of Westerns the studio was making over the next few years. Generally speaking, the group was meant to be heard more than seen, but as time went by, Len (now known as Dick Weston) began to be given small roles of his own. Eventually, he caught the acting bug and decided to try to make his career on the big screen, but when he did a screen test for Universal they felt that he looked too young to portray a real "rootin' tootin' cowboy."

Disappointed, Len continued to work for Columbia until he heard that Republic Pictures was looking for a singing cowboy to build a series of musical Westerns around. He would later admit, "I saddled my guitar the next morning and went out there, but I couldn't get in because I didn't have an appointment. So I waited around until the extras began coming back from lunch, and I got on the opposite side of the crowd of people and came in with them. I'd just gotten inside the door when a hand fell on my shoulder. It was Sol Siegel, the head producer of Western pictures." Rogers auditioned for the role and won a chance to make a screen test. When that went well too, the studio signed him to a seven year contract at a salary of $75.00 a week.

Siegel

For all that he was excited about his new opportunity, leaving the "Sons of the Pioneers" was understandably wrenching. Still, the other Pioneers wished him well, and the four men remained close friends, with Len performing with them whenever he got a chance. He also had to quickly learn that performing in front of a camera was a lot different than performing for an audience, and the studio insisted that he begin an intensive workout to build muscle on to his lean frame. Interestingly, the studio also thought his eyes were too bright, so they had him use eye drops to make them appear less inviting, but when his fans didn't care for the new look, the studio quickly discontinued the practice.

The biggest and most lasting change to Len's life came with the adoption of a new stage name. The studio didn't think Dick Weston sounded like the name of a crooning cowboy, and the quintessential American cowboy, Will Rogers, had passed away recently, so his surname was up for grabs. Leroy Rogers seemed like a great name to the studio executives, but not to Len, who convinced them to shorten it to Roy Rogers.

Rogers worked diligently over the next several years to build his acting career, and his first movie as Roy Rogers was *Under Western Stars* (1938). He also appeared in the Gene Autry film *The Old Barn Dance* (1938), an important step for the young actor because Autry was the biggest Western star at the time. When Rogers starred in *Under Western Stars* (1938), he got to choose his own co-star, a Hollywood horse name Golden Cloud, and he was so impressed with his new mount that he bought the horse for himself and gave him a new name, based on the recommendation of none other than Smiley Burnette, who told him, "Roy, as quick as that horse of yours is, you ought to call him Trigger." According to Rogers, "At first, I trained Trigger and then I met this trainer from Nebraska, Glenn Randall. Glenn was with me for twenty years. Because I'd be on the road with my guitar, I didn't have the time to work with my horse. Glenn came with me and we just worked together on it. I could get Trigger to do just about anything." He would later brag about Trigger, saying, "He could turn on a dime and give you some change." He told another reporter, "I got on him and rode him 100 years and never looked at another horse."

Rogers and Trigger

The movie, with a lot of help from Rogers and Trigger, proved to be a big hit and the first in a long line of musical Westerns they would make together. At first, Rogers tried his hand playing both heroes and villains, including playing the title role in *Billy the Kid Returns* (though his version of the infamous outlaw was much more lighthearted than violent), but whether his characters were good or bad, they always seemed to get the girl. In *Shine on Harvest Moon* (1938), he and actress Mary Hart played out a Romeo and Juliet style story set in the Old West, and Leonard Maltin would later praise the movie, calling it a "Pretty good early Rogers vehicle in which local ranchers suspect that Farnum is still in cahoots with no-good rustler Andrews, even though that partnership broke up long ago…Roy sings two especially nice tunes, 'Let Me Build a Cabin' and 'The Man in the Moon Is a Cowboy.'" Hart would go on to appear with Rogers in a number of movies, including Frontier Pony Express (1939).

Promo picture of Roy Rogers, Lynne Roberts, and Trigger in *Billy the Kid Returns* (1938)

Publicity shot of Rogers and Mary Hart in *Shine on Harvest Moon* (1938).

As Rogers' popularity grew, especially among children who wanted to grow up to be just like him, he began to play good guys exclusively. According to one biographer, "Roy's best known, most frequent characters were of a man that was slow to anger, quick on the draw, and just as quick to forgive." He also began to use his own name for his character, so most of his movies starred Roy Rogers as Roy Rogers. The excitement remained more cheerful than violent, and Rogers soon became a family movie icon. From 1939-1954, Rogers remained on the list of the Top Ten Money-Making Western Stars poll held each year by the Motion Picture Herald. From 1943-1954, he was consistently voted their number one draw, and he kept up similar rankings in polls held by Box Office magazine and other publications. In 1945 and 1946, he was among the Top Ten Money Makers for all movie actors, no matter what the genre.

As his fame grew, Rogers became the actor rising stars wanted to appear with, especially those who aspired to be known as cowboys. In *Dark Command* (1940), Rogers was cast alongside John Wayne to boost the popularity of the movie, and the film also featured one of Wayne's friends, Gabby Hayes. Before long, Hayes would be one of Rogers' most popular sidekicks, and Rogers would later call him "my father, my brother, and my buddy all rolled up in one."

John Wayne in *Born to the West* (1937)

Rogers and Hayes in *The Carson City Kid* (1940)

Chapter 5: World War II

"If I can show our youth what it is like to be a real American, then I'm doing a good job. I want to show them that in this country everybody has a chance—just like I did … In the programs we try to keep everything strictly American and down to earth. That's the sort of thing that will do more to knock any Communist, Nazi, or other such ideas out of their heads than anything else." - Gene Autry

"I think the He-men in the movies belong in the Army, Marine, Navy or Air Corps. All of these He-men in the movies realize that right now is the time to get into the service. Every movie cowboy ought to devote time to the Army winning, or to helping win, until the war is over - the same as any other American citizen. The Army needs all the young men it can get, and if I can set a good example for the young men I'll be mighty proud." - Gene Autry

Though it was becoming increasingly obvious that the United States was on a potential collision course with the Japanese, Autry insisted on continuing to plan for the future. In 1941, he bought a ranch just outside Berwyn, Oklahoma, intending to use it as a breeding and training ground for new stock for his rodeo show. The town was so excited to have a big name movie star living nearby that it passed a resolution to change its name from Berwyn to Autry. Autry himself showed up the day the town officially took his name as its own, and he even broadcast an episode of his radio show from there on November 16, 1941. As it turned out, that appearance would be one of his last public performances for several years.

Following the Japanese attack on Pearl Harbor on December 7, 1941, Congress expanded the Selective Service Code to potentially draft any American man between the ages of 20-44, and in early 1942, Autry learned that he would be among the first to go. He recalled, "I had a friend who worked at the local draft board. He called me and said, 'We're going to have to draft you, Gene.'…So I went to Herb Yates…And Yates said, 'Don't worry about it, hell, they'll never draft you. We'll ask for a deferment on you.' And I said, 'I don't think that would be a good thing, either…For me to ask for a deferment, it would reflect very badly on my behalf, and on yours, too. There's a lot of kids out there on the farm and working in the coal mine, and they're drafting them, and a lot of those parents are going to say, 'How does Gene Autry stay out when my boy is going in?' I didn't want that."

Yates

Thus, on July 26, 1942, Gene Autry was sworn in as a soldier, even if the Army realized he wasn't just any ordinary draftee. In fact, the Army assigned an officer to swear Autry in on the air during a special broadcast of *Melody Ranch*, and the Army also released a statement saying that Autry would be given the rank of technical sergeant and assigned to the Army Air Corps. Though he would not receive an immediate commission like many other stars upon entering the service, he soon earned one, and since he was Gene Autry, he was the only officer ever allowed to wear cowboy boots with his Army Air Corps uniform.

Autry spent much of his first two years in the Air Corps making public appearances at War Bond Rallies and performing for the troops, and after he completed basic training at the Santa

Ana Air Base in California, he was assigned to Luke Field and Thunderbird Field in Arizona. Finally, he reported to Love Field in Dallas to begin his flight training in earnest, where he graduated and received his wings in June 1944. While he was training to learn how to fly, Autry maintained close ties with his Oklahoma ranch, where his cowboys were busy breeding and training horses and other animals that would be used by many of the traveling rodeos that continued to crisscross the United States during the war. In 1943, Autry even signed a formal agreement to provide stock for the World Championship Rodeo Company.

For a time, it looked like Autry would never see combat, and it ended up requiring a favor from Texas Congressman Lyndon Johnson to get him sent into combat. He soon joined the 91st Ferrying Squadron out of Love Field in flying for the Air Transport Command over the infamous "Hump," a dangerous flight path that took him back and forth over the Himalayas between India and China. Autry primarily flew C-109s, hauling fuel to Allied units stationed in China to fight the Japanese, but he also flew some tours via North Africa and the Middle East. During one such mission, while on his way to the Azores, he landed "on a wing and a prayer" after having to reroute his craft five hours to avoid a typhoon. He would remain with the squadron until October 1945.

A C-109 tanker during World War II

In addition to flying, Autry also did what he could to entertain the troops and to keep morale up at home. His exploits were often reported on *Melody Ranch*, now shortened to 15 minutes and renamed *Sergeant Gene Autry* for the duration of Autry's tour of duty. While he was stationed in the United States, he even appeared on the show and also continued to cut and release records. Many of his works during this period spoke to the hearts of soldiers far from home and their loved ones. For example, in 1944, he released the single "I'm Thinking Tonight of My Blue Eyes", with "I Hang My Head and Cry" on the flip side. The following year, he released "Gonna build a Big Fence Around Texas," as well as the cowboy classic "Don't Fence Me In." While these were popular and usually charted for at least a while, it was the heartrending "At Mail Call Today" that shot up to the number one spot on the American music charts.

Autry also tried to keep his fans abreast of his activities with regular letters to his American fan club's newsletter, the *Autry Aces*, but he could not always be as forthcoming as he wanted: "I wish I could share the experiences I have had with you but at the present time the War Department says 'no telling' where I have been or what is going on...Saw several of the boys overseas that I knew. Also met and entertained a lot of the fellows. In fact, almost every place I went, from some place they pulled out a guitar and we had a show; which of course I was very happy to do."

During the last few months of his enlistment, after Japan was defeated but before his discharge could be processed, Autry served with the USO as part of Special Services. Toward the end of 1945, his music began to express the hopes and fears of the soldiers waiting to return home. He created "I'll Be Back," "I Want to Be Sure" and "Don't Live a Lie" in 1945. By the time he was discharged in 1946, Autry had earned the American Campaign Medal, the Asiatic-Pacific Campaign Medal, and the World War II Victory Medal.

While Autry fought in the war, Rogers essentially supplanted him in Hollywood. As Rogers' personal and professional responsibilities grew, he knew he needed to financially plan for himself and Arline, as well as the children they hoped to soon be blessed with. Understanding how little he knew about show business, he hired Art Rush to manage him in 1940, and their contract, which would run for 49 years, was sealed with a hand shake. No legal papers were ever drawn up.

One of the things that Rush was able to accomplish for Rogers was to renegotiate his contract with Republic. When the studio had first hired Rogers, he was an unknown yodeler, but by the end of his first seven year contract, he was, by their own proclamation, the King of the Cowboys. Rush and Rogers thought he deserved more money, but Republic did not want to pay it, so Rush suggested that they would settle for the rights to control and profit from Rogers' name, image, and voice. Republic agreed, unaware that there would be several decades' worth of popular Roy Rogers memorabilia to come in the future. In fact, Rush began working on merchandising quickly by licensing Roy Rogers shirts and hats, as well as bandanas, toy pistols and lassos. During the patriotic years of World War II, mothers rushed to buy their little boys Roy Rogers beds, sheets and blankets, and they encouraged their children to learn to tell time by promising them Roy Rogers clocks and watches. Many kids on the block also wanted to start the new school year off with a Roy Rogers lunch box. Other than items licensed by the Walt Disney Company, Roy Rogers merchandise were be the most popular souvenirs of childhood in America during the '40s.

Part of what made Rogers' merchandise so popular with parents was the wholesome image it portrayed. Rogers was always dedicated to his family, and he insisted that anything bearing his name had to be of the highest tangible and moral quality. For children who could not afford to have his products to enjoy, Rogers also wanted to make sure they could be included by letting them join the Roy Rogers Riders Club, which had no dues. Any child who wanted to join only needed to send a name and address to Rogers, who would then send a "Rogersgram" via "Trigger Express." It would include a membership card for the Roy Rogers Riders Club, along with the club's rules:

1. Be neat and clean.

2. Be courteous and polite.

3. Always obey your parents.

4. Protect the weak and help them.

5. Be brave but never take chances.

6. Study hard and learn all you can.

7. Be kind to animals and take care of them.

8. Eat all your food and never waste any.

9. Love God and go to Sunday school regularly.

10. Always respect our flag and our country.

Though he was not devoutly religious at this point in his life, Rogers believed in good religious training and practice, so when he learned that some children were meeting together for formal club meetings, he wrote a non-denominational prayer for them to open each meeting with:

"Lord, I reckon I'm not much just by myself,

I fail to do a lot of things I ought to do.

But Lord, when trails are steep and passes high,

Help me ride it straight the whole way through.

And when in the falling dusk I get that final call,

I do not care how many flowers they send,

Above all else, the happiest trail would be,

For You to say to me, 'Let's ride, My Friend.'

Amen"

Publicity shot of Roy Rogers and Gail Davis in 1948.

Rogers with Joyce Compton and Phyllis Brooks in *Silver Spurs* (1943)

During his early years at Republic, Rogers remained in touch with the Sons of the Pioneers, and as soon as their contract with Columbia was up, he convinced Republic to hire them too. With that, the quartet began riding and singing across movie screens in America, and beginning with their very first movie together, *Red River Valley* (1941), the group guaranteed every member of their audience a happy ending. The world needed some happy endings, especially as World War II continued to spread across Europe, but Rogers was also personally looking for a happy ending, and at least some happy beginnings too. By 1941, he and Arline had been married for five years but had yet to have a child. Desperately wanting children, they adopted a little girl, Cheryl, in 1941.

Rogers continued to make Westerns, but he made plenty of time in his schedule for Arline and Cheryl. He had grown up in a close, happy family, so he understandably wanted his daughter to have the same experience. Thus, when America joined World War II, Rogers took a different career path than many other actors in Hollywood; even though he was only 30 years old, he did not try to join the military, preferring to stay at home with his wife and young daughter. He also didn't try his hand at making the types of war movies that were so popular during the early '40s.

Instead, he kept doing what he had been doing and built on the success he was already enjoying by making movies that appealed primarily to children and young families.

An image of Rogers, J. Farrell MacDonald and Joan Woodbury from *In Old Cheyenne* (1941)

One thing that made Rogers' movies so popular with children was the fact that they were short. Only after the war was over would any of Roy Rogers' films be more than an hour long. This allowed younger audiences to enjoy the film without having to sit still too long, and it also allowed for the ever-popular double feature that could take up an entire Saturday morning. Another thing that made Rogers' movies special was that they were filmed in color during a time in which most serial Westerns were made in black and white. By 1943, when he was proclaimed the King of the Cowboys, he had a nation full of very young and very loyal fans, and their parents were just as happy with him as their children were because, as Life Magazine put it, "He is purity rampant. He never drinks, never smokes, never shoots pool, never spits...He always wins the girl though he doesn't get to kiss her. He kisses his horse. His immense public would have him no other way."

Rogers was as devoted to his fans as they were to him. In addition to making movies for them, he also spent as much of his free time as possible visiting children's hospitals and group homes. He even taught Trigger to climb multiple flights of stairs so that the horse could join him in these visits, and when he was giving a performance at a club or arena, he always tied Trigger up in front of the venue so that children too poor to purchase a ticket could at least get to pet the world's most famous horse. Rogers' fan base was growing at home as well; in 1943, Arline finally gave birth to a daughter named Linda Lou.

Around this time, Rogers nearly lost his favorite horse when he and Trigger were on their way to a movie set with Rogers in the front seat of the car and Trigger in his horse trailer being pulled behind. Rogers was just coming around a sharp turn when another car barreled toward him in his lane, forcing Rogers to swerve off the road to keep from being hit. As soon as he recovered from his shock, he leapt out of his car and ran back to check on Trigger, and what he saw nearly made his heart stop. There lay Trigger in his overturned trailer, not moving. Seeing the horse's chest rising and falling with each breath, Roy began to speak quietly and soothingly to his old friend while using a rope to gently pull him from the trailer. As soon as he was out of the twisted metal, Trigger opened his eyes and leapt to his feet, completely unhurt.

The only overtly war related movie that Rogers ever appeared in was *Hollywood Canteen* (1943), one of many movies made by Warner Brothers to promote war bonds sales that featured many of the biggest names in Hollywood. The fact that Rogers and the other members of the Sons of the Pioneers were invited to appear in the film indicates just how popular they were at the time, and the group wowed their theatre audiences with a haunting rendition of "Don't Fence Me In," written by jazz legend Cole Porter.

Sons of the Pioneers in *Rainbow Over Texas* (1946)

Autry rides Champion as he's made an honorary member of the Miami Mounted Police.

"There have been several articles in different papers insinuating that I may retire when the war is over, and I want to straighten this out once and for all—I will definitely be back on the screen and on the radio. I am not certain what company I will be connected with, and intend to make bigger and better pictures than I have ever made before. In fact I might produce them myself." - Gene Autry

Throughout his time with Republic, Autry often found himself in conflict with Yates and other corporate executives, but they managed to work out their differences each time, at least in the '30s. However, things changed when he was drafted; the company agreed to put his contract on hold while he was in the Army, but it was not willing to meet some of the other demands Autry made, and he refused to work if his demands were not met. As a result, the war years saw an increase in the adversarial nature of his relationship with Republic, and as the two parties became further estranged, Republic began to promote a new singing cowboy, Roy Rogers, to replace

Autry. By the time the war was over, Rogers was Republic's new man, so after he made a brief return to finish out his contract, Autry was free to pursue other opportunities.

In 1947, Autry wrote the first of several Christmas songs that have remained popular long after his death. It all started in late November 1946 when Autry was invited to ride in the Hollywood "Santa Claus Lane" parade. Autry was just in front of Old St. Nick himself, and as he rode along on Champion, he could barely hear anything over the shouts of children looking past him to the next float and screaming, "Here Comes Santa Claus." Inspired by the event, he came up with some lyrics and had his friend Oakley Halderman compose the melody. Then, Johnny Bond recorded the demo with several other singers, one of whom was holding a cocktail in his hand while singing. The sound of the ice cubes clinking made it on to the recording, and Autry liked the sound so much that when it came time to make the actual single, he replaced the sound of the ice cubes with jingling bells. Following its release, the song "Here Comes Santa Claus" became a huge hit and a perennial favorite in America, covered by everyone from Elvis and Bing Crosby to Alvin and the Chipmunks. As recently as 2013, it was featured on an episode of the hit television series *Glee*.

Children and their moral training continued to be an important part of Autry's life, and during the late 1940s, he published and began to promote a set of moral rules he called "The Cowboy Code". Based on policies he had written to govern how his movies would be scripted and made, they outlined what he considered to be the most important moral rules to live by. According to the code:

1. The Cowboy must never shoot first, hit a smaller man, or take unfair advantage.

2. He must never go back on his word, or on a trust confided in him.

3. He must always tell the truth.

4. He must be gentle with children, the elderly, and animals.

5. He must not advocate or possess racially or religiously intolerant ideas.

6. He must help people in distress.

7. He must be a good worker.

8. He must keep himself clean in thought, speech, action, and personal habits.

9. He must respect women, parents, and his nation's laws.

10. The Cowboy is a patriot.

In 1949, Autry recorded what would soon become one of the most popular Christmas songs ever written. Even today, the song's opening lines are instantly recognizable: "You know Dasher and Dancer and Prancer and Vixen, Comet and Cupid and Donner and Blitzen, but do you recall the most famous reindeer of all…" Based on a storybook originally written in 1939, "Rudolph the Red-Nosed Reindeer" rose immediately to the top of the popular and country music charts as soon as it was released in December 1949. It fell off the chart just as quickly as the holiday season was over, but it has returned to the air every year in the decades since its release

The song was not just a hit in the United States either. Autry would go on to feature it in many of the British tours he began making in 1949, and according to one of his crew members, "He would…encourage the audience to join him in singing RUDOLPH THE RED-NOSED REINDEER which was as big a hit in England as it was in the United States. Gene had worked out a new routine with this, stopping the song to tell the audience to sing louder, suggesting they would be less shy and bashful if the lights were out. He then called to the electrician to douse the lights—to no avail—so he drew his gun and 'shot' the four spotlights out. He said: 'All you boys who brought your girlfriends can leave me one shilling at the box-office when you leave'—and after that the crowd raised the roof with their singing!"

Of course, "Rudolph" was not the only thing that made Autry's tours popular. The *Gene Autry Hit Show* also featured Autry himself, as well as Champion and his "son", little Champ, along with Autry's popular sidekick Smiley Burnette. They were also joined by a variety of other performers through the years, including Gail Davis and The Cass Country Boys. The show regularly filled auditorium with 15,000 or more seats and toured Great Britain each spring and fall for much of the 1950s. This schedule left Autry free to continue making movies during the summer months.

Chapter 7: Roy Rogers and Dale Evans

Dale Evans in 1944

"When I first met Roy, I thought he was rather shy--quite good looking, but rather shy." - Dale Evans

"'Cowgirl' is an attitude really. A pioneer spirit, a special American brand of courage. The cowgirl faces life head-on, lives by her own lights, and makes no excuses. Cowgirls take stands; they speak up. They defend things they hold dear." – Dale Evans

Though Rogers' movies typically had a female lead cast opposite him, it was not an easy role for an actress to play, given that her chance to shine would come after the singers and even Trigger. Once Mary Hart was tired of playing those parts, Rogers had a hard time finding someone else who was willing to appear with him, at least until a young actress named Dale Evans was cast opposite him in *The Cowboy and the Senorita* (1944). Though she didn't want the role any more than the other actresses it was offered too, she agreed to play it to the best of her ability. She even learned to ride a horse, though Rogers observed that he "saw a good deal of sunlight" between her and her mount during the first scene. While there was nothing romantic between the two, they soon became good friends and began to make film after film together.

In 1944, Rogers also launched *The Roy Rogers Show*, a 30-minute radio program that aired on more than 500 stations across the United States. Though it would evolve over time into a more dramatic series, in its early years it consisted primarily of Rogers singing songs in a format based loosely around a storyline. According to radio historian John Dunning: "The early shows followed the pattern set by (Gene) Autry's Melody Ranch...Rogers' show featured Roy and the Sons of the Pioneers in such fine Western favorites as 'Tumbling Tumbleweeds,' 'Cool Water,' and 'Don't Fence Me In.' Much of the show was campfire banter and song, with Roy and songstress Pat Friday doing vocal solos, Perry Botkin leading the Goodyear orchestra and Verne Smith announcing. Dramatic skits were offered, but leaned to lighter material than what the show used in later years. Ultimately, it became primarily a Western thriller show." The Roy Rogers Show would be broadcast on radio for eleven years.

For a while it seemed that Rogers' life could not get any better. His movies were raking in money and, more importantly to him, making people happy. The war ended in 1945, just months before Arline announced that she was expecting another baby, and he also released his first musical single, the haunting "A Little White Cross on the Hill." But around this time, Evans broke the news to him that she was leaving Republic Pictures to join another studio that had promised her the starring role in a musical comedy. While it is impossible to know, and Evans herself never admitted it, one cannot help but wonder if she had developed romantic feelings for her leading man, whom she knew was happily married.

Tragically, Rogers would not remain happily married for much longer. In October 1946, Arline woke Roy to tell him she was in labor, and after driving her quickly to the hospital, he joined the other fathers pacing in the maternity floor waiting room before being told that he had a son. Mother and baby, whom they'd already agreed would be named Roy Rogers Jr., were doing well. As was the practice at that time, Arline would remain in the hospital to recover while Roy went back to work, visiting her and his son in the evenings, but just a few days before Arline was to be discharged, Roy got a shocking call informing him that Arline was very ill and he should come to the hospital immediately. It turns out that she had developed a blood clot following the birth and it had broken lose, travelling to her brain and causing an embolism that soon burst. She died that evening as Roy held her hand and begged God to spare her.

After arranging for his beloved wife's funeral, Roy hired a nurse to care for the baby, whom he called Dusty, and his two toddler girls. He continued to make movies, knowing that he had to support his family, and it was also a welcome break from his children's constant questions about when their mother was coming home. Life in the Rogers home went on, and every one slowly began to heal.

One thing that Rogers felt deep in his heart was that, no matter his own feelings, his little children needed a mother. While he was not interested in entering the dating scene around Hollywood, he began to keep his eyes open for some woman that he felt could fill at least some of the gap left by Arline's death. As fate would have it, Rogers ran into Evans again in early 1947, this time in Atlantic City while he was making a personal appearance and she was on tour. She had heard about Arline's death and offered him her condolences. Needing a friend during this trying time, Rogers invited her to return to making movies with him, but while Evans was sympathetic to his plight, she was not interested in returning to the role of Roy Rogers' girl sidekick. The musical she had hoped to make when they had parted had been shelved, and she was still looking for another one.

However, several bad movies later, she accepted his offer, and the two were back in the saddle again. Rogers also released his most popular single, "My Chickashay Gal", in 1947, a song that topped out at fourth place in the American Country Music Charts. From that time on, their romance moved way too fast to just be known as a whirlwind. According to Evans, "In the fall of 1947, we were booked at the rodeo in Chicago. We were on our horses in the chutes, waiting to be introduced to the audience, when Roy said, 'Dale, what are you doing New Year's Eve?' New Year's Eve was still months away. I had no plans. Then he reached into his pocket and pulled out a small box. Inside it was a gold ring set with a ruby. He put the ring on my finger and said, 'Well then, why don't we get married?'" Before she could give him an answer, Trigger noticed his cue and reared up before making a galloping entrance into the arena. Out of habit, her own horse, Buttermilk, followed close on Trigger's heels. But Evans was not about to make Rogers wait for her answer either: "Before lifting the microphone to sing the national anthem, I turned to look at Roy. He looked back at me, beaming with delight. The din of cheers made it impossible to speak. I formed the word Yes' with my lips. He nodded, and we began to sing."

Thus, Rogers and Evans were married on New Year's Eve 1947. They were both in their mid-30s, and between them they already had four children, though Evans' oldest son was an adult whom she had given birth to when she was only 15. Their quiet wedding, held at the Flying L Ranch owned by their friends Bill and Alice Liken, was nearly cancelled because of a snowstorm that blew into Davis, Oklahoma that night. The minister who was to perform the ceremony could not drive his car out to the ranch, so he eventually had to arrive on horseback. Then, when the minister had finally arrived and Rogers headed downstairs to meet his bride, a bright light coming from an upstairs bedroom caught his eye. A fire had broken out, so he and his best man, Art Rush, beat the fire out and threw the burning curtains into a bathtub full of water while

Evans sat downstairs waiting for her groom to arrive.

While their marriage would ultimately be a happy one, it got off to a rocky start, primarily over issues of faith. Not long after their wedding, Evans became a born-again Christian, a decision that Rogers respected but was not crazy about. While he believed in God, he had not forgiven or forgotten the loss of his first wife, so Evans was welcome to practice her faith as long as she did not try to rope him into it. Over time, Rogers noticed the hope and joy that Evans' beliefs brought to her and how it affected the way she treated him and their children, so he also began considering making a similar commitment to Christianity. He finally converted in 1949.

In addition to their faith, Rogers and Evans continued to share their love of acting by starring together in five movies in 1949 and 1950: *Susanna Pass (1949)*, *Down Dakota Way (1949)*, *The Golden Stallion (1949)*, *Bells of Coronado (1950)* and *Trigger, Jr. (1950)*. The last ones were certainly bittersweet, as it introduced a younger replacement for the aging Trigger. He had become too old and temperamental to make a good performing horse and was given a well-deserved retirement in the pasture behind the Rogers' home, where he spent his days in the company of other horses and pets, not to mention the Rogers children. Trigger would also soon be joined by Evans' horse, Buttermilk, with whom he had starred in so many movies, and Trigger occasionally came out of retirement to appear with Rogers and Evans on their television show.

Meanwhile, Rogers' singing career continued to keep pace with his movie making. In 1950, he released a solo single, "Stampeded," which went to the 8th spot on the country music charts in America. It would be the last solo single that he made, but two decades later he would see a resurgence in interest in his music.

Not long after his conversion, Rogers and Evans found that one of their most fervent prayers had been answered. Though she was now 38, Evans became pregnant, and Rogers again found himself in the expectant fathers' waiting room. Eventually, he got the good news that the baby had arrived, but this time, the tragedy came much sooner; just hours after he learned that little Robin had been born, the doctor asked to speak with him and Evans privately. He explained that the infant girl had been born with Down's Syndrome, a barely understood condition that would leave her physically and mentally fragile. The doctor advised Rogers and Evans that rather than take their daughter home to her waiting nursery, they should place her in an institution where she could be cared for by experts.

The doctor must have been taken aback when Rogers said no, but it's understandable that a man who had already lost his wife would not want to lose a newborn daughter. Thus began a two year challenge that ended when Robin died just two days short of her second birthday. Though short, her life changed the lives of not just Rogers and Evans but their entire family, and Evans would later write the Christian best-seller *Angel Unaware*, a book that changed the lives of people across the world and inspired new and better treatment of children with Down's

Syndrome.

Rogers' experience with Robin also strengthened both his faith and his commitment to his family. He began to introduce Christian hymns into his programs, including singing "How Great Thou Art" in Madison Square Garden. Though his promoters were initially concerned that these additions would hurt his popularity, they actually made him more popular, and his 43 performances at the Garden broke all former attendance records. Rogers also made five movies in 1951 while Evans stayed home with Robin, and this would be his last full year of acting. He appeared in *Spoilers of the Plains (1951), Heart of the Rockies (1951), In Old Amarillo (1951), South of Caliente (1951)* and *Pals of the Golden West (1951)*. Evans joined him on screen for the last two times in *South of Caliente* and *Pals of the Golden West*.

Back at home, he and Evans knew that while she would not be able to have any more biological children, they still wanted a larger family. The first child that they were interested in was a Native American baby named Mary Little Doe, but when they expressed an interest in adopting her, they were first turned down. The law in the State of Texas, where she was living, said that only parents with some sort of Native American heritage could adopt a Native American child, so everyone was pleasantly surprised when Rogers produced the necessary paperwork to prove that his maternal great-grandmother had been a Choctaw, a member of the same tribe as Mary Little Doe. The adoption was completed and the two took their new daughter home, soon nicknaming her Dodie.

Not long after Dodie's adoption was complete, Rogers and Evans were in Cincinnati, Roy's hometown, for a performance. As they usually did, they invited a group of children from the local orphanage to be their guests at the show, and when the children arrived, Rogers himself went out to meet them. It was then that a thin little boy about his own sons' age sauntered up to him, put out his hand, and said with a big smile, "Howdy partner." Roy was entranced and insisted that Dale should meet the five year old. They agreed that he would make a wonderful addition to their family and began the adoption process the next day. A few months later, they returned to Cincinnati to take Sandy home with them to California.

Chapter 8: Television Cowpokes

Autry and the Pinafores, who performed with him on his radio show in the 1940s

"I think my biggest thrill, as far as TV is concerned, was the reception my first TV film received from the public and the critics. I was one of the first movie people to make a film especially for television, but if I had listened to many of my friends, I never would have ventured into TV films. They told me I was making a big mistake by going into a new field and that I had better stick to regular feature-length movies. I must confess I wasn't sure myself just what reception my first TV picture would have." - Gene Autry

Beginning in 1950, Autry also managed to find time to work on a weekly television series, *The Gene Autry Show*, with each week's show featuring a different story that starred him. One week, he might be a sheriff, while he might be a rancher the following week, and his sidekick on the show, Pat Buttram, later went on to achieve fame as the double-dealing shyster Mr. Haney in the popular television show *Green Acres*. Autry directed the series himself and produced it through his "Flying 'A' Production Company", which made him the first movie star to produce his own television show. The first four seasons of the show were shot primarily in black and white, but the last season was filmed in color, and each episode ended with Autry's own theme song, "Back in the Saddle Again". Following the end of the show in 1955, it was replaced for 26 episodes with a spin-off entitled *The Adventures of Champion*. Like *The Gene Autry Show*, it was based on the radio series by the same name.

Autry in an episode from *The Gene Autry Show* entitled "The Black Rider"

Many episodes of both television series were filmed on the Melody Ranch (originally the Placerita Canyon ranch), which Autry purchased in 1952 and named for his own popular radio show. Autry once mentioned the history of the location: "When I bought the old Melody Ranch, as I called it, from Monogram Pictures, it had been used for the filming of hundreds of Western movies with stars like Harry Carey, Johnny Mack Brown, Bob Steele, Tom Tyler and many more. My first feature picture for Republic Studios, *Tumbling Tumbleweeds*, had been filmed at the Placerita Canyon ranch in 1935. Years later, in 1958, John Wayne and I worked there together for the first time in a television special called 'The Western' for the NBC series *Wide, Wide World*."

Autry, who never intended to use the ranch for anything other than movie making, soon sold off most of the 110 acres, retaining only the 12 acres that included replicas of a Western town, adobes and a ranch cabin. He also held on to enough land to allow him to shoot long shots of cowboys galloping across the range. In addition to providing the backdrop for many of his own movies and other Westerns, Melody Ranch was also used as the setting for the earliest years of the iconic television show *Gunsmoke*.

Ironically, Autry would make few of his own movies at the ranch. At first, he didn't envision that there would be a problem making movies and the series at the same time, saying, "I can't see any conflict between television and the movies. They each will create a demand for the other. The thing I like most about television is that much shorter shooting schedule for TV pictures. I like this better than the longer drawn out shooting schedule of regular length movies." However, he soon learned otherwise; in fact, he filmed his last movie, *Last of the Pony Riders* (1953), just a couple years after he purchased the set.

By 1954, Autry's television series had risen to such popularity that it caught the eye of a critic from *The New York Times*: "The gentleman leading the cowhand invasion of color TV had been none other than Gene Autry…If his caliber on tinted image can be attained with a film made over two years ago, as Mr. Autry's was, the future success of 16 mm color picture can hardly be questioned…Just a little puzzling, however, were the amazing recuperative powers of the cast. Mr. Autry and the evildoers could 'slug' each other madly but when it was all over there was not a hint of a discolored cheek. Possibly Champion also will not be too happy over color TV. In one household the loudest whistles were heard for a honey blonde. It's going to be the ladies, not men and horses, who will benefit most from color TV."

Though he no longer needed horses for rodeos and movies, Autry remained interested in raising horses for the rest of his life, so in 1954, he purchased a top bucking string and hired Harry Knight, a Canadian with a good reputation for raising horses, to run it. Two years later, he bought out the World Championship Rodeo Company and merged it with his own venture, after which he moved the stock from both units to a huge ranch outside of Fowler, Colorado. Over the following decade, Autry's ranch would provide most of the animals used in rodeos touring much of the Southwest. He continued to appear in rodeos himself even after he sold the company in 1968 and was inducted into the Pro Rodeo Hall of Fame in 1979.

Though he enjoyed his work with horses, Autry's passion still lay with traveling and performing, and his work on two continents was recognized in an article that ran in the *Boston Herald* in 1954: "One of America's best diplomats is Gene Autry. Through the medium of his radio show, he is doing a great deal to help Great Britain and the United States understand each other. In a very simple way, he has helped us to use our own interests to gain understanding…Perhaps Gene Autry with a guitar and a horse can do more than pacts and treaties to bring two peoples together."

Autry and Gail Davis in Toronto

In 1950, Autry agreed to record yet another holiday song, but this time it was for Easter. "Here Comes Peter Cottontail" had been written the previous year by Steve Nelson and Jack Rollins, but they asked Autry to record it, and when the recording was released by Columbia, it reached the Number 3 spot at the height of its popularity. It remains one of the most popular Easter songs of all time and led the three men to record "Frosty the Snow Man" the following Christmas. That hit reached the Number 7 spot on the United States Pop Charts. Autry made his final new holiday record in 1953 when he recorded "Up on the House Top," a song written nearly a century earlier by Benjamin Hanby of New Paris, Ohio. Though the song would be recorded by many different singers, Autry's version has remained the most popular.

Fittingly, Rogers was transitioning into television around the same time as Autry. With five children at home, Rogers and Evans wanted to move away from the grueling schedule of making movies, so they turned their professional efforts to television. When Rogers' contract with Republic was being renegotiated in 1951, he learned that the studio would not allow him to work on television because they intended to trim his movies down to 54 minutes and market them as a type of television Western series. However, since he wanted to make his own series with Evans, he refused to give them the rights to his name and image, which he had retained in earlier contracts. By this time, the name Roy Rogers and his likeness were much more valuable than the movies themselves. Angry and disappointed, the studio fired him, and aside from an uncredited appearance in *Alias Jesse James* (1957), Rogers would appear in only one other movie, the made-for-TV family film *MacIntosh and T. J.* (1976). Like Autry had earlier, Rogers had come to learn how difficult it could be to do business with Herb Yates, but years later, Rogers still refused to speak ill of the owner of Republic, telling one reporter, "I don't want to talk about Yates. Let's just say he wasn't very flexible."

Once Rogers was done with Republic, he and Evans threw themselves into developing *The Roy Rogers Show*, which premiered on December 30, 1951, the day before their fourth wedding anniversary. The show ran for 100 episodes before being cancelled in 1957, but by then, Roy Rogers and Trigger, along with Dale Evan and Buttermilk, had galloped across nearly every television screen in America. They were also joined by another Rogers family member: Bullet the Wonder Dog, a smart German Shepherd who was always ready for adventure. The show aired on Sunday evenings and always ended with the sweet sounds of Rogers and Evans singing,

"Happy trails to you, until we meet again.

Happy trails to you, keep smilin' until then.

Who cares about the clouds when we're together?

Just sing a song and bring the sunny weather.

Happy trails to you, until we meet again."

According to one critic writing a review in 1954, "Both radio and television versions of Western stories, starring the King of the Cowboys, tell the exciting tales of the West in which Roy is aided in maintaining justice and order in the mystical town of Mineral City by his human friends Dale Evans, Pat Brady, the Sheriff and his animal friends, Trigger, the palomino horse, and Bullet, a highly intelligent police dog."

Chapter 9: Life and Death in Apple Valley

Rogers and Evans performing at Knott's Berry Farm in the 1970s.

"I've been interviewed by just about every newspaper or magazine down through the years. I just tell it the way it is or how it's been. I had an ordinary family life, really." - Roy Rogers

As his children got older, Rogers found himself looking for ways to spend more quality time with them, and one of the things most important to him was that they share his love for the outdoors. Thus, he bought a motorboat to take Dale and the children out on local lakes to fish and swim, and while out on the water, he developed an interest in boat racing. He began entering motorboat races, tweaking his engine himself at first and then later hiring a mechanic to help him get the most power from his engines. Much to his surprise, he soon learned that he had the skill and equipment to win races.

In the 1950s, the idea that children should be kept away from guns was still all but nonexistent, and since Rogers had grown up with a rifle in his hand, he also wanted his children to learn to shoot as well. He often took them and their friends hunting for venison, wild boar, pheasant, and even bear, and he later took the family on two African safaris and a hunting trip to Alaska. That said, Rogers preferred to avoid killing anything he did not plan to eat, so he began taking his family to skeet shooting events, and before long, he decided to try his hand at the sport. As with boating, Rogers not only enjoyed skeet shooting but discovered he still had the sharp eyes and steady hands that he needed to win some awards.

While most tourists bring home souvenirs from their travels abroad, Rogers and Evans brought home another child, a girl named Mimi who they met while performing in Great Britain in February 1954. While touring Scotland, the couple visited an orphanage where the 13 year old had lived for most of her life. Charmed by the child, they asked about adopting her, only to learn that her parents were still alive and would not surrender her. Her parents did agree, however, for her to visit America with the famous movie stars. The visit became longer and longer until the parents finally agreed that Mimi could remain in the United States as the Rogers' legal ward.

In 1955, Rogers and Evans brought home their last child, a little Korean girl named Deborah Lee, whom they called Debbie. At three years old, she was considered unadoptable by her Korean orphanage because her father was a Puerto Rican who had been stationed in Korea as part of the United Nations' forces. Now with a total of 7 children aged between the ages of 3 and 13 at home, Rogers and Evans were busier than they had ever been before. Always a team, they shared both parenting and performing obligations equally, and whenever possible, they took the children on tour with them, with the entire family occasionally appearing on stage to sing and play instruments. In time, the world fell in love with the entire family, but when at home, the parents and children stayed busy with school, church, and personal activities.

Sadly, it was one of these wholesome activities that would reintroduce tragedy to Rogers and his family. In 1964, Roy and Dale, always anxious for their children to share their blessings with others, agreed to let Debbie, who had just turned 12, join a church youth group taking toys and clothing to an orphanage in Tijuana, Mexico. While they were on their way home, the bus carrying the kids crashed, injuring many of the kids and killing Debbie and her best friend. Shocked, Rogers clung to his faith and his family, but he barely recovered from Debbie's death before he lost another child. When Sandy had joined the military in 1964, his parents were thrilled to learn that he would be sent to Germany instead of Vietnam, but Sandy died suddenly in his sleep in 1965. For Roy, Dale, and the rest of the family, the pain was familiar but nearly unbearable; they had now lost three children, burying three of the people who should have lived to bury them.

In 1960, Rogers became one of a handful of performers to have three stars on the Hollywood Walk of Fame, one each for Motion Pictures, Television and Radio, but after Sandy's death in

1965, Rogers and Evans decided to make a change. Their three oldest girls, Cheryl, Linda and Mimi, were all married and starting families of their own, and Dale and Roy wanted to get away from Hollywood and raise their remaining children in a place that looked more like the small towns in which each of them had grown up. There was no need for either of them to continue to act, as their family could live quite comfortably on the money generated by the sale of Roy Rogers memorabilia, and the two didn't want to act anymore. As Rogers told one reporter during the mid-1960s, "Today they're making pictures that I wouldn't take Trigger to see." In later years, he would look back on this period with a certain wistful sadness, saying, "The world changed. Hollywood changed. I think we've lost something, and we don't know how to get it back."

Having retired from making movies, Rogers and Evans purchased a small hotel in Apple Valley, California. At first, they thought they might enjoy being innkeepers, but they soon learned that it was more effort than it was worth. Though now in his 50s, Rogers was still in good health, and he wanted to open a museum where he could showcase his life and faith in a way that would inspire other families. He explained, "Not long after Will Rogers died, they turned his ranch into a museum. And it didn't have anything in it. So I made up my mind I was gonna keep everything." Thus, he and Evans bought a large ranch house near Victorville, California and moved their entire brood out there. They also purchased a rundown bowling alley in Apple Valley and turned it into the Roy Rogers-Dale Evans Museum. There was no problem furnishing the museum, because, as Rogers explained to a reporter, "After so many years in show business, I thought it was a good idea to have a museum for the people. It's stuff that I've saved all my life. I came up during the Depression when we never had anything. Every time I got something, I'd just hang on to it. When we first opened the museum, I had two tractor trailer loads of things."

One of the main attractions at the museum was the famous Trigger. When the horse died in 1965, Rogers had decided that he should keep him around, explaining, "I just couldn't think of burying old Trigger. Too many people loved him. We took Trigger, Dale's horse Buttermilk, and Trigger Junior and had them beautifully mounted. Trigger is up on his hind legs and he looks just like he did the day before he died." Later, Rogers would add, "When I die, just skin me out and put me up on old Trigger and I'll be happy." Another attraction was the Slye family car that had survived the long trip to Hollywood.

In 1968, Rogers secured another source of income for his family when he licensed his name to the Marriott Company for use in their new Roy Rogers chain of restaurants. Though that was the extent of his involvement, the restaurants have flourished for decades and are still around today, with each restaurant featuring a photograph of Rogers on one of its walls.

Ironically, the same cultural revolution that drove Rogers from filmmaking brought about a resurgence of interest in his music. The conservative backlash against the hippie movement led many to develop a passion for all things traditional and wholesome, and what could be more traditional and wholesome than Roy Rogers, a man who only ever kissed his horse or his wife on screen, and one who wrote prayers and co-authored Christian books? Rogers himself must have been pleasantly surprised when he was approached about recording an album of some of his favorite songs. Though *The Country Side of Roy Rogers*, released in 1970, was not a big moneymaker, it did make the country music charts in the United States and sold well enough to justify making *A Man from Duck Run* the following year. His second album did better than the first and, after a brief hiatus, Rogers and Evans made *Happy Trials to You*. Released by 20th Century Music in 1975, it featured their most popular signature duets.

Meanwhile, the Rogers' Museum was outgrowing its original home and needed a larger location, so Roy approached his son Dusty, who had become a general contractor, and asked him to build a new, larger facility to hold the collection. Thus, the Roy Rogers-Dale Evans Museum re-opened in Victorsville in 1976, and while the taxidermied Trigger was displayed indoors, along with similarly stuffed Buttermilk, Roy had an even larger-than-life statue of Trigger cast to stand on top of the building. The statue of the rearing horse could be seen from more than 1,000 feet away when the museum opened.

As such details suggest, Rogers was very much a hands-on museum owner. He would often show up unannounced to shake hands with his fans and have his picture taken with them, and he never seemed to tire of signing autographs or offering a big smile and kind words for everyone he met. People were often surprised at how little he seemed to have aged from the way they remembered him when they were children, and unlike many stars, he never seemed to expect any sort of preferential treatment or adulation. In fact, Rogers seemed as excited to meet the men and women visiting his museum as they were to meet him. When asked about his fame, he would typically reply modestly, or as he once put it very mildly, "I did pretty good for a guy who never finished high school and used to yodel at square dances."

In 1976, Rogers and Evans became one of only a few married couples to be inducted together into the Western Performers Hall of Fame at the National Cowboy & Western Heritage Museum in Oklahoma City, Oklahoma. Nearly two decades later, in 1995, Rogers was inducted into the Hall a second time as a member of the "Sons of the Pioneers".

In 1988, Roy Rogers became the first person to ever be inducted into the Country Music Hall of Fame twice, and to this day he remains the only one. The first time was in 1980, when he was inducted with the other members of the Sons of the Pioneers. Then in 1988 he was inducted in his own right. In support of his induction, one Nashville columnist wrote, "Two generations of Americans grew up with Rogers on the silver screen, TV and radio - and the impact he had on the present success of country music would be hard to estimate and easy to underestimate." When Rogers released his final studio album, *Tribute*, in 1991, it went higher in the Country charts than any of his previous albums, topping out at an impressive 17th place. Rogers also made his first and only music video, teaming up with popular country star Clint Black to create "Hold On Partner" in 1991.

Rogers remained in good health well into his 80s, and though he would have loved to remain active riding, roping and making public appearances for the rest of his life, he did know that aging brought new limits. In his later years, he told a reporter, "When you're young and fall off a horse, you may break something. When you're my age, you splatter." However, in 1996, he began to fade, developing congestive heart failure that made it difficult to breathe and left him unable to walk very far. He died on July 6, 1998 at his home in Apple Valley, California with Evans and his living children by his side, as well as some of his grandchildren. After a Christian funeral led by the pastor of his local church, he was buried at the Sunset Hill Memorial Park in Apple Valley. Evans would be buried by his side three years later.

In a tribute written years after his death, one reporter summed up his legacy almost perfectly: "He gave us standards to live by that helped teach us the difference between right and wrong. His willingness to stand up for the things he believed in inspired us. And his religious faith and his concern for the less fortunate helped mold our character. Roy lived his life off camera with the same decency and humility that he projected on television and on the silver screen. He was the hero who never let us down. Despite all the success that came to him, Roy never seemed to lose his way. And he never forgot that his fans were the ones who made it possible for a poor boy from Ohio to attain a level of success greater than anything he could ever have imagined. His decency and strength of character come from a simpler time in America."

Autry in Miami for the premiere of his movie *Texans Never Cry*

"If your youngster has a faith to live by he'll never wander off the trail. As any cowhand can tell you, it's easier to keep 'em on a well-marked trail than to hunt for a maverick when he's wandered away. Even when you find 'em they don't always want to come back. It's like that with youngsters. Give them a trail to follow—something to guide them when problems come along—and you'll never have a maverick on your hands. Even when the grazing looks greener away from the path, if your kids are sure the path leads to something - even though they can't see the destination—they'll stick to it. It's all in believing—in having faith. I guess that's the biggest gift any parent can give a child—and it's more valuable than anything money can buy." - Gene Autry

Gene Autry was one of the biggest names in show business for nearly 20 years, but like every other star, his career inevitably began to decline, and unfortunately, Autry joined many other stars in turning to a bottle for comfort when it happened. By 1956, he had developed a real problem that made it difficult for him to work, and in order to get a handle on the situation, he decided to take time off and quit drinking altogether. After a number of weeks taking care of himself, he told a reporter, "I took a whole month's vacation—my first ever...As a result, I've never felt better in my life. I have always enjoyed my work so much that it never occurred to me that taking time away from it could be enjoyable. Matter of fact I always wondered why anyone would want to take a vacation if he honestly liked what he was doing. Now I know that a little let-up once in a while does a man a lot of good. I hope I'll be able to get another vacation—in, say, ten years or so."

Actually, Autry got a much longer vacation sooner than he thought, at least at the time of that interview. Though he was not yet 50, Autry began to think about retirement during the mid-1950s, and he made one final appearance at the Melody Ranch in 1958 in a television special showcasing Western movies. A few years later, in 1961, Autry retired from traveling with his road shows.

In 1962, Autry suffered a personal tragedy that would change his plans and those of many others in Hollywood when he lost his precious Melody Ranch to fire. Elvis Presley, who was in the area for a photo shoot, help fight the blaze by throwing buckets of water on one burning building and saved the house used for the exteriors in the Mae West/W. C. Fields classic *My Little Chickadee* (1940). Though most of the structures were lost, two locomotives from the early 20th century survived, and Autry subsequently donated them to two historical museums in the area.

More than anything else, Melody Ranch was meant to be the retirement home of Autry's beloved Champion, but after the fire, Ina Autry stepped in and arranged for an old friend, Henry Crowell, to come in and care for the horse. Autry himself would only visit occasionally, and he later reflected on the immense damage done in the blaze: "When a fire all but devastated Melody Ranch in August 1962, what I lost could not be replaced or even measured. The ranch was in the path of the terrible firestorm that raged through the San Gabriel Mountains...I had always planned to erect a Western museum there, but priceless Indian relics and a collection of rare guns, including a set used by Billy the Kid, went up in smoke. Thank God, the ranch hands and all fourteen of our horses were uninjured. The fire left the terrain so convincingly battle-scarred that it was used two months later for an episode of television's war series, *Combat*...I have been back only a very few times. I kept it until the last living Champion died (in 1990) and then sold it to two enthusiastic young men, Renaud and Andre Veluzat, who decided to rebuild it."

Autry had always been a shrewd businessman and continued to invest his money well, even after his retirement. Though he was no longer making movies, he still had a number of things he wanted to do with his life, and he was fortunate enough to have the time and the money to do them. Moreover, many honors came after Autry's retirement. On February 8, 1960, he had the unique experience of being the recipient of 5 different stars on the Hollywood Walk of Fame, one each for Motion Pictures, Radio, Recording, Television and Live Performance. To this day, he remains the only performer in history to have five stars on the Hollywood Walk of Fame.

Autry earned similar awards over the next few decades as well. In 1969, Autry was inducted into the Country Music Hall of Fame, and the following year, the Nashville Songwriters Hall of Fame welcomed him into their illustrious halls. In 1972, Autry was inducted into the Western Performers Hall of Fame, located at the National Cowboy and Western Heritage Museum in Oklahoma City, Oklahoma. In 1980, he was voted into the Hall of Great Westerners at the National Cowboy and Western Heritage Museum, and he was inducted into the Oklahoma Hall of Fame in 1991.

In 1961, Autry finally realized one of his lifelong dreams when he purchased a newly formed professional baseball team, the Los Angeles Angels. It all started the previous year when Autry heard that there was a new baseball team forming, and he approached Major League Baseball executives and asked if he might buy the rights to broadcast the team's games on the radio. The executives liked his style and persuaded him to buy the team instead. He would remain an owner until his death in 1998, at which time the number 26 (for the 26th team member) was retired in his honor.

Autry spent much of the early 1970s working on his autobiography with the help of author Mickey Herskowitz. *Back in the Saddle Again* detailed his life from his childhood in Texas to his retirement when it was published in 1976, and Autry also released record albums that year. *South of the Border, All American Cowboy*, and *Cowboy Hall of Fame* all featured many of the songs he had made famous during his career, even if none of the albums were particularly well received. Two years later, in 1978, Johnny Cash recorded a hit song entitled "Who is Gene Autry?" While promoting the song, Cash asked Autry to autograph his famous Martin D-35 guitar, and Cash later showed it off in one of his own final music videos for the song "Hurt".

Though he had supported Lyndon Johnson in his early years, Autry became increasingly politically conservative during the years following Johnson's presidency. In 1977, the Freedoms Foundation awarded him the American Patriots Medal, and he joined fellow conservative actors Charlton Heston and Mickey Rooney in 1995's docudrama *America: A Call to Greatness*.

A 1993 picture of Autry on the set for on the set of *America: A Call to Greatness* (1995)

Throughout his life, Gene Autry was happily married, so naturally, the death of his wife Ina in 1980 was a huge blow. Unable to face living out the rest of his days alone, he married Jacqueline Ellam shortly after, and they remained together until his own death.

Among Autry's many investments through the years were a number of country and western radio stations. In 1982, he sold one of these, KTLA in Los Angeles, for $245 million. He later sold off KSFO in San Francisco and KOGO in San Diego, as well as KMPC in Los Angeles, taking the money he made from these sales to finance his dream of opening a museum honoring the lives and work of the diverse peoples of the West. He later noted that it fulfilled a dream he had once thought lost with the destruction of Melody Ranch: "My plans for a Western museum … came to fruition with the opening in 1988 — after much hard work spearheaded by my wife Jackie and Joanne Hale — of the Autry Museum of Western Heritage, located in Griffith Park opposite the Los Angeles Zoo." Today, the museum not only honors Autry's life but contains more than 21,000 artifacts, including pieces of visual and tactile art, clothing, textiles, guns, tools, playthings and musical instruments from all the different peoples that shaped the West through their lives and work. It also strives to be culturally sensitive to Native American populations and expand a modern sense of understanding of their heritage and lifestyles, and the museum is particularly proud of its outreach programs for children, a demographic Autry always valued.

Displays of souvenirs owned by Autry at the Autry National Center

Autry enjoyed good health well into his 80s, but in the later stages of the 1990s, he was diagnosed with lymphoma. Gene Autry was 91 when he died of lymphoma at home in Studio City, California on October 2, 1998. Following his funeral, he was interred at the Forest Lawn Hollywood Hills Cemetery in Los Angeles.

Bibliography

Autry, Gene (1978). *Back in the Saddle Again.* New York: Doubleday.

Cusic, Don (2010). *Gene Autry: His Life and Career.* Jefferson: McFarland.

Enss, Chris and Kazanjian, Howard (2005). The Cowboy and the Senorita. Guilford, CT: Globe Pequot Press.

George-Warren, Holly (2007). *Public Cowboy no. 1: The Life and Times of Gene Autry.* New York: Oxford University Press.

Green, Douglas B. (2002). *Singing in the Saddle: The History of the Singing Cowboy.* Nashville: Vanderbilt University Press.

Guyot-Smith, Jonathan (1998). Paul Kingsbury, ed. *The Encyclopedia of Country Music*. New York: Oxford University Press. pp. 22–23.

Kazanjian, Howard (2005). Happy Trails: A Pictorial Celebration ... Guilford, CT: Globe Pequot Press.

Magers, Boyd (2007). *Gene Autry Westerns*. Madison, NC: Empire Publishing, Inc.

Phillips, Robert W. (1995). Roy Rogers: A Biography. Jefferson, NC: McFarland.

Rogers, Roy; Morris, Georgia (1994). Roy Rogers: King of the Cowboys. New York: Collins Publishers.

and Dale Evans (1994). Happy Trails: Our Life Story. New York: Simon & Schuster.

and Carleton Stowers (1979). Happy Trails: The Story of Roy Rogers and Dale Evans. Waco: Word Books.

Made in United States
North Haven, CT
13 May 2024

52433746R10043